A very special thanks to all the farmers!
This includes all the workers who help in the planting,
pruning of the grapevines, and harvesting of the grapes
that are dried as raisins. This also includes the
transporters and distributors who make sure raisins are
available to people around the world.

About the Author

Karen Adler, a classroom educator for twenty-one years, has her MA in Curriculum and Instruction from Fresno Pacific College. She has always emphasized the importance of agriculture and its role in our everyday lives.

Awareness of the relevance of science, history and social sciences is Ms. Adler's goal with all her students. Nutrition is another area she emphasizes.

Karen Adler lives in North Fork, California with her husband Jim, and their two dogs, Mona and Bub.

Books by Karen Adler:
Insects and Spiders.   Evan-Moor Publishing, 1995
Letters from Whitey.   Karen Adler Books, 2000
Maybe Donna Wants a Cheeseburger!
    Karen Adler Books, 2004
California Grapes.   Karen Adler Books, 2005

About the Illustrator

Tawn R. Morrison is a graduate of Ohio University, where she majored in Education and minored in Art. She also received her MA from the University of Pittsburgh. She taught in the field of Gifted and Talented Education for twelve years. Her love of art is evident in the illustrations found in *The Mouse and the Rock, a Metaphor, Maybe Donna Wants a Cheeseburger!, A Story About Raisins*, and in the upcoming Adler Animal Anthology: *"Whooo, Me?"*

Tawn lives with her husband Kelly and two children, Tristan and Megan, in Fresno, California.

To:

From:

Date:

Love,
Karen
Allen

Published in North Fork, California
Karen Adler Books
Copyright © 2005

Printed by Jostens in Visalia, California
ISBN 0-9679772-4-X
website: karenadlerbooks.com

A Story About
Raisins

Written by
Karen A. Adler

Illustrated by
Tawn R.Morrison

1

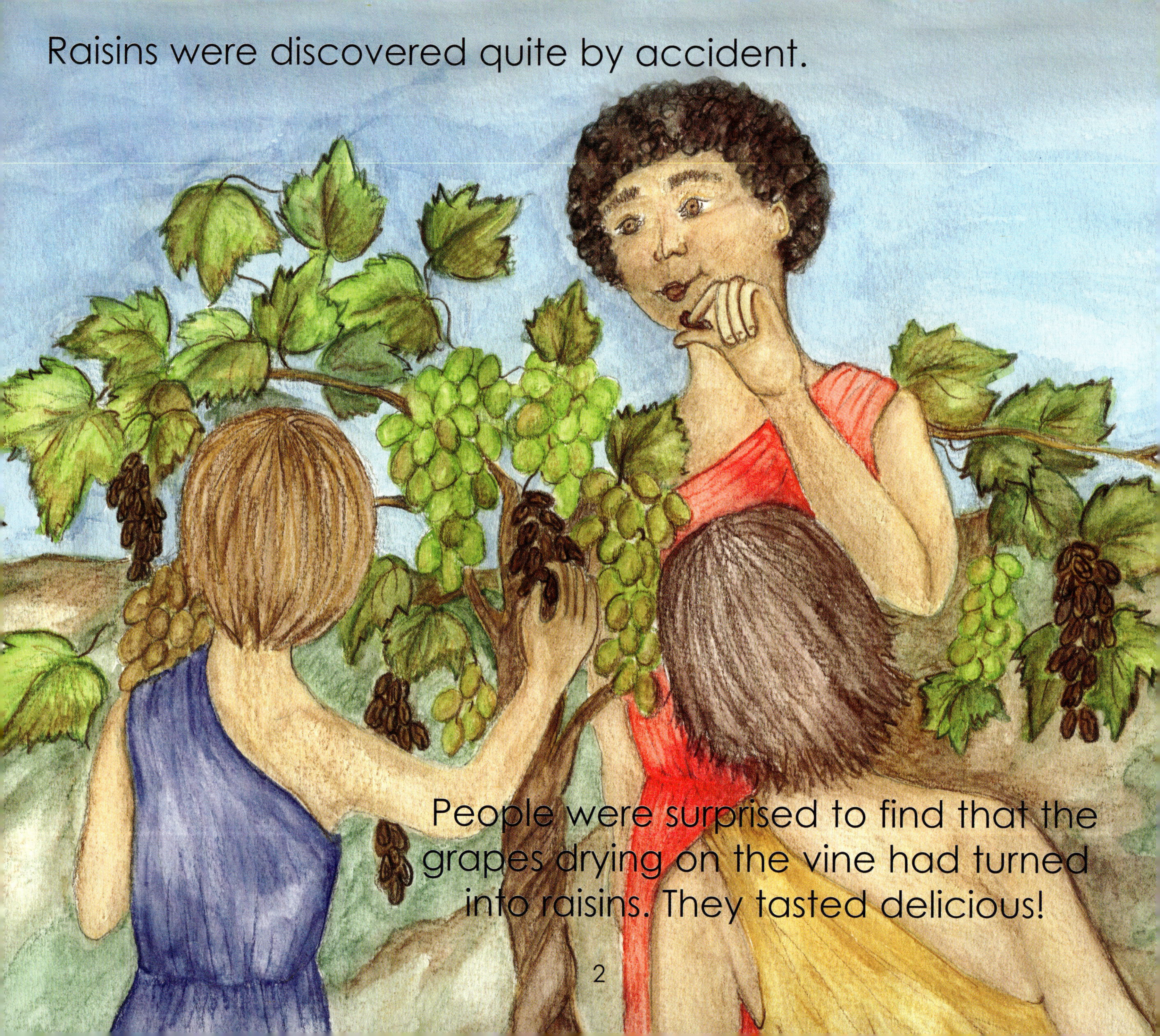

Raisins were discovered quite by accident.
People were surprised to find that the grapes drying on the vine had turned into raisins. They tasted delicious!
2

The first people to dry and sell raisins lived in Spain, Greece and Persia.

Because raisins were dried,
people took them everywhere.
Even ancient warriors
carried raisins across
the Alps.

4

The knights loved raisins, too.
They shared them with everyone they met.

5

Raisins are made from grapes.

The sunshine helps the grapes dry.
When grapes dry, they turn into raisins.

Some raisins are cut from the vine
then dried on trays.

Other raisins are dried on the vine.

9

California is the best place to grow raisins
because of its dry, hot weather.

Most of the raisins grown for the
world today come from California.

Raisins have many nutrients that can
help keep you healthy and strong.

Raisins can also make you feel younger.
They give you energy.

No matter where you live, you can enjoy eating
that wonderful little gift from nature–raisins!

Try these fun and nutritious recipes made with raisins.

Ants on a Log

Ingredients:
4 stalks of celery
4 Tablespoons of peanut butter
1/4 cup raisins

Directions:
1. Spread 1 Tablespoon of peanut butter on a stalk of celery.
2. Sprinkle some raisins over the peanut butter.
3. Now eat your ants on a log!

This recipe makes four servings.
Each serving contains approximately
120 calories.

Raisin Faces

Ingredients:
4 rice cakes
4 Tablespoons of peanut butter
1/4 cup raisins

Directions:
1. Spread 1 Tablespoon of peanut butter on the top of a rice cake.
2. Use 1 Tablespoon of raisins to make a face on the rice cake (eyes, nose and mouth).

This recipe makes four servings.
Each serving contains approximately
145 calories.

Raisin Fruit Salad

<u>Ingredients:</u>
1 apple (chopped into small pieces)
1 orange (peeled and chopped into small pieces)
1/4 cup raisins
1/4 cup chopped almonds
4 ounces low-fat yogurt (any favorite fruit flavor)

<u>Directions:</u>
1. Mix all ingredients together in a large bowl.
2. Spoon into small cups or bowls.

This recipe makes four servings.
Each serving contains approximately
150 calories.

Raisin Trail Mix

Ingredients:

1/4 cup raisins

1 cup of dry cereal (cheerios, puffed rice, corn or wheat cereal)

1/2 cup coarsely chopped almonds

1 cup dried apricots (or other dried fruit of your choice) cut into small pieces

Directions:

1. Mix all ingredients together in a large zip-lock bag.
2. It's now ready to eat right out of the bag!

This recipe makes four servings.
Each serving contains approximately
250 calories.

Try adding raisins to these foods:

On top of yogurt

On top of hot or cold cereal

Add raisins to shredded carrots
mixed with a little bit of mayonnaise

Oatmeal cookies made with raisins

Pancakes sprinkled with raisins

Rappin' Raisin Song

I'm a little raisin,
I used to be a grape
'til dried in the sun
from our beautiful state.

Discovered quite by accident
a long time ago,
a heat wave settled in
and wouldn't you know?

Those grapes started dryin'
right there on the vine,
and when the people tried them,
they found them quite divine!
<u>Chorus</u>
I'm a rappin' raisin
hear me when I say,
I was born long ago
but I'm here to stay!
So pop me in your mouth
I'm tasty and sweet.
No matter where you take me
I'm ready to eat!

Words by Karen A. Adler
Copyright © 2005

Can you answer these questions about raisins?
(Answers on next page)

1. Raisins were first discovered how many years ago?________.

2. Ancient warriors could carry raisins long distances because they were____________.

3. Raisins are made from__________.

4. What helps the grapes dry?____________.

5. Some raisins are cut from the vine then dried on_________.

6. Other raisins dry on the_________.

7. Why is California the best place to grow raisins?____________.

8. Raisins are very nutritious.   They help give you ____________.

Answers

1. Raisins were discovered **thousands of years ago**.

2. Ancient warriors could carry raisins long distances because they were **dried**.

3. Raisins are made from **grapes**.

4. The **sunshine** helps the grapes dry.

5. Some raisins are cut from the vine, and then dried on **trays**.

6. Other raisins dry on the **vine**.

7. California is the best place to grow raisins because of its **dry, hot weather**.

8. Raisins help give you **energy**.

Visit Karen Adler's website at:
karenadlerbooks.com